Phonics Tales!

Teaching Guide

Lessons, Activities, and Reproducible Versions of All 25 Storybooks

by Judy Nayer

New York • Toronto • London • Auckland • Sydney
New Delhi • Mexico City • Hong Kong • Buenos Aires

Teaching Resources

Cover design by Maria Lilja
Interior design by Grafica, Inc.
ISBN: 0-439-88455-1

Table of Contents

The Mini-Books

Short Vowels

Long Vowels

Other Vowels

Blends and Digraphs

A Note to Teachers

Many factors play a part in the process of learning to read. As a teacher, you want to give your students all of the essential tools for reading success. Research shows that phonics, or the relationship between sounds and their spellings, is an important element of reading instruction.

Why is phonics so important? In the first stage of learning to read, children pay more attention to contextual cues, such as context and picture clues. They may be given stories with rhyming and repetitive patterns that help them predict text. They also may memorize most words by sight. These strategies become insufficient, however, when the number and variety of words increase. That is why during the second stage of reading, students focus on sounding out the letters in words. In order to sound out words, readers must be able to associate a specific spelling with a specific sound. That's where phonics instruction comes in. By teaching this relationship between sounds and their spellings, children's decoding skills strengthen and they can begin to identify words quickly and accurately. Only then can children move on to the third stage of learning to read, the automatic stage, when readers use both phonics and meaning cues and are able to read with greater speed and fluency.

Approximately 84% of English words are phonetically regular. Therefore, teaching the most common sound-spelling relationships is extremely useful. It means that with good phonics instruction, children are able to sound out most of the words in their oral vocabulary. With practice, word recognition becomes more and more accurate. Equipped with strong decoding skills, children are able to devote more mental energy to reading comprehension. Indeed, research shows that phonics instruction, as part of a balanced reading program, can make a difference between reading failure and reading success. By teaching children how to unlock the mysteries of print, you can help them discover the joy of reading and send them on their way to becoming lifelong readers.

For phonics instruction to be effective, it needs to be taught in context rather than in isolation. The *Phonics Tales* program was created to help you combine the teaching of phonics with connected text. Each of the 25 stories focuses on a different phonics element, or sound-symbol relationship. The *Alpha Tales* program began the reading journey with letter recognition and beginning consonant sounds. Now, the journey continues with short and long vowels, vowel pairs, consonant blends and digraphs, and other common phonics elements. By devoting an entire book to a single sound, you can immerse students in language that targets the sound/spelling you are studying. This kind of focus can serve to heighten children's awareness of language and spelling patterns and accelerate learning. The words in each story that contain the target phonics element are in bold type. This feature helps to focus children's attention on specific words and invites them to interact with the text.

Reading *Phonics Tales* is an engaging way for children to apply their developing phonics skills while listening to enjoyable stories. The series can be an effective tool in enabling you to:

- ❖ help children learn and reinforce common sound-spelling relationships
- ❖ reinforce and build upon children's phonemic awareness skills (the awareness that words are made up of different sounds)
- ❖ support children's oral language and listening skills
- ❖ help children build vocabulary
- ❖ help children build decoding and word recognition skills
- ❖ help children learn spelling and writing skills

The instruction that accompanies the *Phonics Tales* series is tailored to help you maximize the benefits of each book in the program. This instruction focuses on teaching children to distinguish sounds, match letters and sounds, and read and write words. Suggestions include:

- ❖ listening activities to discriminate sounds in words
- ❖ manipulation activities to change the sounds and letters in words
- ❖ blending activities to help children sound out words
- ❖ word-building activities to help children make words
- ❖ practice reading and writing words using the phonics elements children learn

Children need many experiences with language and literature as they learn to read, and many different materials are needed to make up a balanced reading program. We hope the *Phonics Tales* series becomes a valuable part of your phonics and reading toolkit that helps you meet the needs of all your beginning readers. Remember, as you read the stories to your students, always show your excitement and interest in the written word. A love of reading is one of the most important things you can share!

Welcome to Phonics Tales!

Learning to read is an exciting and important accomplishment for any child. Nothing can be more important than teaching children the skills they need to become successful, lifelong readers. Learning phonics—the relationship between letters and sounds—is an essential part of opening the door to the wondrous world of books.

Phonics Tales offers a fun and effective way to capitalize on children's natural interest in learning to read and speed up their reading progress. Each playful, imaginative read-aloud story in the *Phonics Tales* collection introduces children to a new phonics element, such as short *a*, long *o*, and the blend *ch*. The program contains one book for each of 25 important phonics skills, including short vowels, long vowels, variant vowels, consonant blends, consonant digraphs, and more. The engaging stories provide opportunities for children to apply their developing phonics and decoding knowledge, while providing a joyful and language-rich reading experience.

Here are features of the *Phonics Tales* program that will help to capture the fun and excitement associated with learning to read:

❖ A riddles activity at the end of each story that invites children to answer ten riddles using words with the featured phonics element (see page 15 of each storybook)

❖ An easy-to-learn rhyming cheer designed to help children recite and remember key words that include the target phonics element as well as to celebrate learning (see page 16 of each storybook)

❖ Teaching notes, assessments, and activity suggestions to help you introduce each *Phonics Tales* book, build on each story's phonics lesson, strengthen children's reading and decoding skills, and monitor students' progress (see pages 7–20 of this teaching guide)

❖ Reproducible patterns for making mini-book versions of all 25 stories in the *Phonics Tales* series (see pages 21–120 of this teaching guide)

Using the Program

Learning About Letters and Sounds

As you help children develop their knowledge of phonics, or the relationship between letters and sounds, keep in mind the following:

❖ Two prerequisites for learning to read are 1) the ability to recognize the letters of the alphabet quickly and in random order, and 2) phonemic awareness ability, or understanding that words are made up of different and discrete sounds. Check children's abilities in both areas. For phonemic awareness, see if children can orally blend sounds. Say the sounds of a word, pausing between each sound or group of sounds. For example, say /m/ . . . *at.* Ask children to orally blend the sounds to make a word (*mat*). Use the storybooks and the activities in this teaching guide to continue to reinforce and develop children's phonemic awareness skills.

❖ Review and reinforce the beginning and ending consonant sounds and letters as you teach the short vowels presented in this program. Begin with simple words, focusing on three-letter short-vowel words with the C-V-C (consonant-vowel-consonant) pattern. Also, have children manipulate the consonant letters in these words. For example, have children change the *m* in *mat* to an *s* to make the word *sat.*

❖ The example words in the stories vary from short and simple words to more difficult and sometimes multisyllabic words. The rich language serves to enhance children's awareness of the target sounds and letters and boost their vocabulary and language skills. It also makes for a more enjoyable and engaging story. When encouraging children to read the target words on their own, begin with simple words made up of phonics elements they already know. Then, allow children to progress to more difficult words at their own pace.

Using the Storybooks

Before Reading

Introduce the featured phonics element of the *Phonics Tales* book you are reading with an assortment of quick activities.

❖ Read aloud the title of the book. Have children use the title and the cover illustration to make predictions about what the story will be about. Flip the book over and read the story summary on the back cover. Were children's predictions correct?

❖ Introduce the phonics element shown on the cover of the book. For example, for the book *That Cat Max*, introduce the short-*a* sound. Explain to children that the letter *a* is a vowel that spells the /a/ sound as in the word *cat*. Write the word *cat* on the chalkboard and have a volunteer circle the letter *a*. Help children recognize that the /a/ sound is made by the letter *a*. Ask children to suggest other words that contain /a/.

❖ Have children listen as you read the title again. Ask them to name all the words in the title that have the target sound.

❖ Tell children that this book has lots of words with this sound and that the words are in boldface type. Skim the book with children and look for words containing the phonics element. Have children point to a few of them as you read them together. Run your hand under each letter as you blend each word aloud. Say and hold each sound in the word, blending the sounds together. For example, for the word *Max*, you would say, "MMMMMaaaaaxxxxxxxxxx." Then have children repeat the word.

During Reading

❖ The first time, read the selected *Phonics Tales* book aloud all the way through. Let children enjoy the story and get a feel for the language.

❖ When you reread the story, ask children to look and listen for words with the featured phonics element—the words in boldface type. Let children signal when they see and hear these words. Also, pause to read the Phonics Fact each time one appears and have children answer any questions posed.

❖ On another reading of the story, ask children to closely examine the illustration on each page. Do they see anything pictured whose name contains the phonics element? Can they find words in the illustration and in the speech balloons?

❖ After several readings, encourage children to chime in on predictable words, especially words containing the phonics element. You may need to pause before the word as you point to it to help children sound it out. Have volunteers work through blending words with the phonics element, starting with simple words and progressing to more difficult ones. Children will delight in seeing how many words they know and can learn!

❖ Additional options for reading include reading the story chorally, having volunteers read a page at a time, or having partners read the story independently.

After Reading

❖ Allow children time to reflect on what they liked about the story and to share any other comments they have. Ask questions that focus on their understanding of the story and their attention to words containing the target sound.

❖ Share the page of riddles at the end of each *Phonics Tales* book. Challenge children to answer the riddles by reading the words in the Word Box and choosing the correct word. Read the words in the Word Box aloud if necessary. Write more words with the target sound on slips of paper. Have children take turns choosing a word and creating riddle clues for it until the class guesses the word.

❖ Have fun with the cheer that accompanies each *Phonics Tales* book. After reciting the original cheer, let students make up a new cheer. Write the cheer on chart paper, leaving blanks for each word that includes the target phonics element. Have children take turns filling in the blanks to complete the cheer. Make mini-megaphones out of rolled up paper. Shout it out!

❖ Play a quick game to reinforce the target phonics element. For example, if you're teaching the blend *fl*, say the sound for *fl* and then say a word that starts with *fl*, stretching out the initial sound. Let children take turns saying other words that start with that sound, also stretching out the beginning.

Using the Mini-Books

The reproducible mini-books are an excellent way to strengthen children's reading skills and build a home-school connection. Here are some ideas for using the mini-books both in and out of the classroom.

❖ After you've read a *Phonics Tales* story aloud several times, provide children with the reproducible mini-book pattern and help them make their very own copy of the story. Children can then follow along in their mini-books as you read the story again. Model decoding strategies along the way—for example, say a word in parts to model oral blending: /f/ /a/ /n/, or /f/ . . . *an.*

❖ Make audio recordings of the stories and put them in a special listening center. Provide copies of the mini-books so that children can follow along with the tapes.

❖ As you teach each phonics skill, create a mini–learning center where students can gain additional practice recognizing and writing words with the sound/symbol correspondence. The mini-books can form the basis of one learning center activity. Simply place copies of the mini-book in the center, and have children read and write the words in the story that include the target sound.

❖ Ask each child to bring in a shoebox from home. Then set out a variety of art materials and allow students to decorate the boxes. Children can then use the boxes to house their very own *Phonics Tales* mini-books. Children will enjoy returning to the stories again and again.

❖ Let children take home their mini-books to read with family members. The more practice children have with the phonics elements in words, the more familiar they'll become with using those elements to read and write new words. Sending the mini-books home for students to share with families is one way to provide this practice. Children can "announce" the phonics element your class is currently studying by wearing a special badge. The badge can also serve as an invitation to parents and caregivers to read the latest *Phonics Tales* story with their child. Children and adults can then look around their home (on food labels, the mail, magazines, and so on) for more words with the featured sound.

Making the Mini-Books

1 Make double-sided copies of the mini-book pages. (You should have two double-sided copies for each one.)

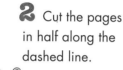

2 Cut the pages in half along the dashed line.

3 Position the pages so that the lettered spreads (A, B, C, D) are faceup. Place the B spread on top of the A spread. Then, place the C and D spreads on top of those in sequence.

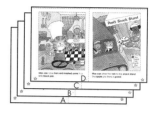

4 Fold the pages in half along the solid line. Make sure all the pages are in the proper order. Staple them together along the book's spine.

Making the Badge

Photocopy the pattern for each child. Trim the badge to size and help children fill in the featured phonics element. Children can then color the badge. Punch a hole at the top and string with yarn so children can wear the badge around their neck.

This week
we're studying

_____

(phonics element)

**Let's read the *Phonics Tales*
mini-book together.**

Assessment

The following assessments will help you evaluate children's progress with the phonics skills presented in the *Phonics Tales* program. These assessments are cumulative in nature and are to be used after each group of *Phonics Tales* books: short vowels, long vowels, other vowels, and blends and digraphs. Each assessment is designed to be used individually. Make two copies of the assessment to be given. Give one to the student and keep the other to record each child's errors. As the child reads aloud the words, record his or her attempts, corrections, errors, and passes. Use the assessments to help determine whether children have mastered these skills and which skills need more reinforcement. (You may use the activity suggestions on pages 17–20 to provide additional work with skills children have not yet mastered.)

The following questions will also help you assess each child's reading skills. Ask yourself:

- ❖ Does he/she recognize the phonics element in words?
- ❖ Can he/she read words with this element?
- ❖ Can he/she spell words with this element?
- ❖ What is the degree of automaticity, or speed, with which he/she can accomplish these tasks?

Student's Name _____

Have children read the following word list.

cat	six	red	but	mop
hug	fan	big	job	pen
not	lip	duck	tap	wet
yes	mud	lap	pot	did
hat	hen	odd	gum	pig

Student's Name _____

Have children read the following word list.

ape	like	bee	cute	hole
huge	race	mine	road	meet
roll	kind	need	lake	mule
five	cube	rain	rose	tea
see	race	toad	kite	use

Student's Name _____

Have children read the following word list.

room	side	her	found	star
sound	bird	zoo	fork	cape
turn	soon	house	robe	urn
horn	use	car	moon	loud
mouse	side	cool	out	fort

Student's Name _____

....

Have children read the following word list.

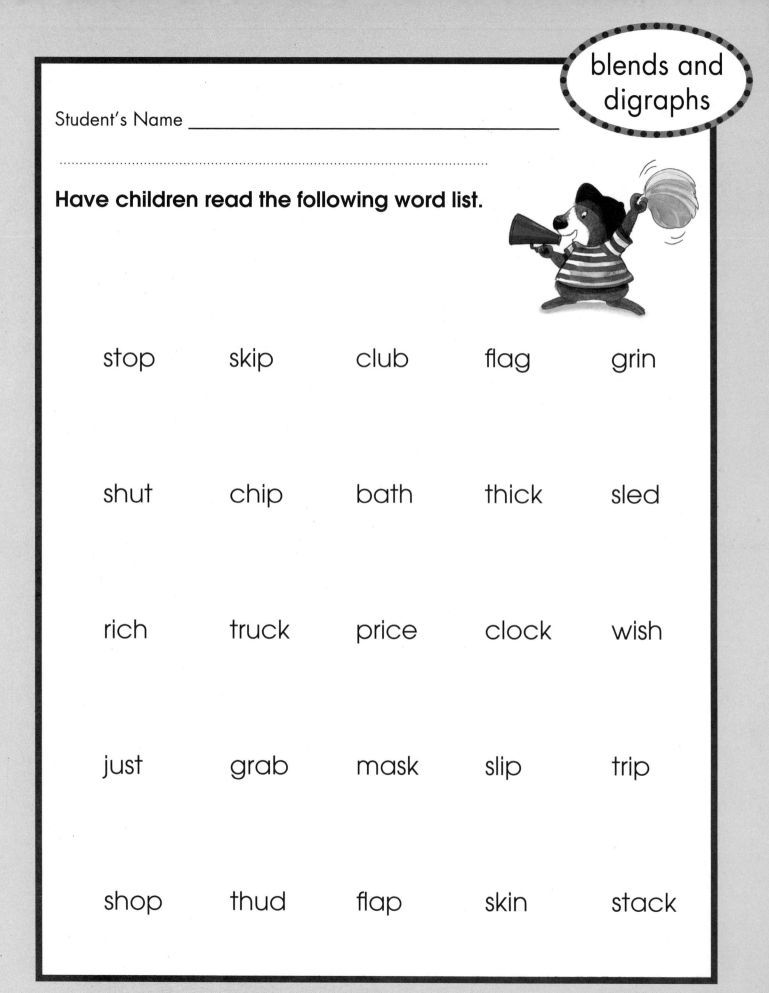

stop	skip	club	flag	grin
shut	chip	bath	thick	sled
rich	truck	price	clock	wish
just	grab	mask	slip	trip
shop	thud	flap	skin	stack

Phonics Games and Activities

Use these activities to further reinforce and provide hands-on experiences with the phonics elements introduced in the *Phonics Tales* books.

Phonics Tales Word Wall

Use the *Phonics Tales* stories to build an interactive word wall that supports students in phonemic awareness, understanding letter-sound relationships, decoding, and more. Start by writing the phonics element on a large sheet of craft paper. After sharing the story once, reread it, asking children to listen for the words that include the target phonics element. Write the words on the word wall and draw pictures to go with them. For sounds with spelling variations, list words in separate columns according to spelling. Let children add to the word wall on their own; they can use the books to help spell words or ask you for help. Revisit the word wall often to read new words. Invite volunteers to take turns creating sentences with the words.

Phonics Tales Around the Room

Each time you read a *Phonics Tales* story, invite children to search around the room for items with the target sound. Have children write the name of the object on a sticky note and place it on the object. You can also give children clues, such as, "I spy something that begins with the blend *cl*. It's hanging on the wall. It tells the time." (clock) When you are finished working with the story, collect the sticky notes and place them on index cards. Add these to your collection of word cards.

Climb the Word Ladder

Copy and distribute the reproducible Word Ladder on page 18 of this teaching guide. On the chalkboard, begin a word ladder by writing a three-letter word, such as *cat*. Then, invite children to climb the word ladder by changing one letter in the word to form a new word. Show children an example by filling out a word ladder with the following words: *cat, can, ran, run, rug, hug*. Explain that the beginning consonant, ending consonant, or vowel can be changed, and underline the new letter each time. For more of a challenge, you may wish to work with four-letter words. For example: *name, fame, face, race, rice, mice*. Always get children started by giving them the word for the first rung of the ladder. Have children work on their own or with partners.

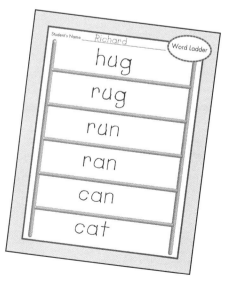

Student's Name _____

Tongue-Twister Fun

Students will quickly notice the alliterative language in the *Phonics Tales* stories for blends and digraphs. Reread a sentence from the story you are using, and ask students what sound they hear repeated at the beginning of some of the words. Write the sentence on the board and invite a volunteer to underline the beginning letters that are the same. Make up a tongue twister after sharing one of the stories. For example, for *Shelly's New Shoes* you might write the following: "Shoeless Shelly shopped for sharp, shiny shoes". Say it once slowly and then invite children to say it quickly. Have them make up their own tongue twisters and write them on the board. Have children recite each other's tongue twisters. You may also wish to record them on an audiotape for listening fun.

Pop Up for Words

Review the featured phonics element for the *Phonics Tales* story you are sharing—for example, long *i* from *Ike* and *Mike*. Write words that contain the sound on index cards. List the same words on a piece of paper. Have children sit in a circle, and give each child a word card. Explain that when they hear their word they are to pop up on their feet and hold up their card. After all the cards have been read, collect, shuffle, and redistribute them and play again. Encourage children to see if they can improve their speed.

Listen Up!

Reinforce children's phonemic awareness skills with a variety of quick listening activities, such as the following:

❖ Tell children that you are going to say some words that have the sound you are studying—for example, *sl* from *Sleepyhead Sloth*. You'll also say a word that doesn't belong. When they hear a word that doesn't belong, they are to say "Buzzzz!" For a variation, gather children in an open area and invite them to run around as you shout out words that have the same phonics element. When they hear a word that doesn't belong, they should "freeze."

❖ For vowels, make and distribute letter cards for *a, e, i, o,* and *u*. Tell children you are going to say a word with a short vowel. Have children hold up the letter that represents the vowel sound in the word you say. On another day, repeat for words with long vowels.

❖ For digraphs, tell children that you are going to say some words, and they are to tell you if they hear the featured sound at the beginning or at the end of the word. For example, when /sh/ is the featured sound, if they hear /sh/ at the beginning, they should put their finger to their lips and say "shhh." If they hear /sh/ at the end, they should put their hands together and wiggle them like a fish.

❖ For multisyllabic words, tell children you are going to say some words and they are to clap to show how many syllables, or word parts, they hear in each word. For example, if you say the word *pencil*, they will clap twice—*pen . . . cil*. Say the words slowly, sound by sound. Use words from the stories.

Silly Sentences

Write silly sentences on the board, in which the underlined word is one or two letters from being the correct answer. Ask a volunteer to change the letter(s) to form a word that will make sense in the sentence. Have the child erase the old word and write the new word in its place. Continue with other sentences, using words from the story you are working on. See the examples below.

> Lucky Duck had pancakes for <u>branch</u>. (brunch)
> The trolls traveled by <u>grain</u> to the lake. (train)

Storytime Fun

Have children make their own class books based on the *Phonics Tales* stories. For example, ask children to make a page for a class *That Cat Max* book, using the sentence starter "That cat Max _____." Have each child complete the sentence, including at least one word with short *a*. Suggest that the children draw a picture to go with their sentence. Provide a few examples:

> That cat Max likes ham and yams.
> That cat Max can rap and tap and clap.
> That cat Max naps in my lap.

Beanbag Games

Arrange children into two or three teams. Divide a big sheet of drawing paper into five sections. Write a vowel in each section. Then challenge children to a beanbag toss. Have team members take turns tossing the beanbag onto the paper. When the beanbag lands, have the child say the letter in that section and also think of a word that has that short vowel sound. Write the words on the chalkboard, keeping separate columns for each team. Players earn one point for each new word. The team with the most points at the end of the game wins. Play again with long vowels and other vowel sounds.

To review blends and digraphs, arrange children in a circle. Pass around a beanbag, and say a chant, such as "Round and round we go. When I stop, stay a word that begins like truck." The child who is holding the beanbag when you finish the chant must say a word with the same beginning sound.

Short-a Cheer

Hooray for short *a*, the best sound around!

Let's holler short-*a* words all over town!

There's **map** and **plant** and **rap** and **cat**.

There's **pan** and **band** and **stamp** and **hat**.

There's **man** and **grass** and **jazz** and **tap**.

There's **act** and **fast** and **snap** and **clap**.

Short *a*, short *a*, give a great cheer,

For the **happiest** sound that you ever will hear!

Make a list of other short-*a* words. Then use them in your cheer.

Phonics Tales!

short a

That Cat Max

by Liza Charlesworth
illustrated by Stephen Lewis

■SCHOLASTIC

. . . is **nap** on my **lap**. **Man**, I love **that cat Max**!

I'm **having** a **blast**!

Max can play **catch**.

I **am** a **fan** of **that cat Max**. Why?

Short-a Riddles

Listen to the riddles. Then match each riddle with the right short-*a* word from the box.

Word Box

fast	grass	cat	tap	jam
nap	acrobat	hat	can	subtract

1 This pet says, "Meow!"

2 It is the opposite of *slow*.

3 This is a lot like jelly.

4 It is the opposite of *can't*.

5 Sleepy babies do this in a crib.

6 You put this on your head to keep warm.

7 It is green and grows in backyards.

8 A person who does gymnastics is called this.

9 It is the opposite of *add*.

10 A kind of dancing that makes a lot of noise.

Answers: 1. cat 2. fast 3. jam 4. can 5. nap 6. hat 7. grass 8. acrobat 9. subtract 10. tap

Daffodils

Pansies

Max can cut the **grass**.

But the best thing **Max can** do...

Max can even **act** like **an acrobat**!

Max can chat with **Sandy Blat** about her **brand**-new **tan hat**.

Max has talent! He **can tap and rap**.

Max can do **math**! He **adds and subtracts** super **fast**!

Phonics Fact

Sometimes the short-*a* sound comes in the second syllable of a word, such as sub**tracts**.

Max can do **crafts**. He made **that fancy basket**.

C

Max can also play **sax** in my **dad's jazz band**.

Max can cook **ham and mashed yams** in a little **black pan**.

D

Max can drive the **van** to the **snack stand**. The **apple** pie there is **grand**!

Short-e Cheer

Hooray for short *e*, the best sound around!

Let's holler short-*e* words all over town!

There's **west** and **next** and **red** and **hen**.

There's **net** and **fresh** and **nest** and **men**.

There's **best** and **bench** and **shelf** and **send**.

There's **mess** and **spell** and **yes** and **end**.

Short *e*, short *e*, give a great cheer,

For the most **elegant** sound you ever will hear!

Make a list of other short-*e* words. Then use them in your cheer.

16

Phonics Tales!

short e

The Best Nest

by Liza Charlesworth
illustrated by Kelly Kennedy

SCHOLASTIC

"I **bet** my **nest** is the **best** in the **West**," said **Jen**.
"**Yes**! **Yes**!" agreed **Ben** and **Bess**.
They were so **impressed**!

14

One day, **Jen** decided to **get** her own **nest**.
She packed a **chest** with the **help** of her **parents**,
Ben and **Bess**.

Phonics Fact
Sometimes the short-*e* sound comes in the second syllable of a word, such as in par**e**nts.

3

Phonics Fact

The letter *e* is a vowel. A vowel can make a short sound. The short-*e* sound is found in words such as **red**, **hen**, and **Jen**. What other short-*e* words can you find in this story? Look at the pictures, too!

This **red hen** is named **Jen**.

A

Short-e Riddles

Listen to the riddles. Then match each riddle with the right short-*e* word from the box.

Word Box				
yes	pen	bench	wet	red
shell	hen	bed	nest	ketchup

1 This is the word for a *girl chicken*.

2 A strawberry is this color.

3 You might search for one at the beach.

4 It means the opposite of *no*.

5 You put this on french fries.

6 A bird builds one in a tree.

7 Pigs live in this place.

8 You sleep on one at night.

9 It means the opposite of *dry*.

10 You can sit on this at the park.

Answers: 1. hen 2. red 3. shell 4. yes 5. ketchup 6. nest 7. pen 8. bed 9. wet 10. bench

Our little **red hen** is all grown up!

Jen pecked them good-bye. Then she **set** out **west** to find the **best nest**.

B

Jen served an **elegant** meal of **fresh** worms and **ketchup**.

Then, **Jen** invited her **very** first **guests**.

Jen saw a pig **pen** and **went** inside. But that **pen** was a **mess**! It was not the **best nest**.

Jen made **them** into a **nest**.

This **shed** is a **wreck**!

Jen saw a **shed** and **went** inside. But the **shed** was **bent** and **let** all the rain in! **Jen** got very, very **wet**.

Jen saw a **tent** and **went** inside. But the **tent** belonged to **ten elves**! It was not the **best nest**.

6

Next, **Jen** built a **desk** and a **bench** and a cozy **bed** for taking a **rest**.

11

Phonics Fact
A word can have more than one short-*e* sound. The word **excellent** has three!

It was **definitely** not the **best nest**. Then, Jen got an **excellent** idea.

8

Phonics Fact
Sometimes the short-*e* sound is made by the letters *ea* as in **thread**. Can you find another *ea* word on this page that makes the short-*e* sound?
(Answer: **feathers**)

Jen found sticks and **stems** and **shells** and **thread** and **feathers** and even some **french** fries.

9

Short-i Cheer

Hooray for short *i*, the best sound around!

Let's holler short-*i* words all over town!

There's **pig** and **trip** and **wish** and **miss**.

There's **lip** and **fish** and **drink** and **dish**.

There's **skip** and **milk** and **six** and **big**.

There's **pink** and **chimp** and **dish** and **wig**.

Short *i*, short *i*, give a great cheer,

For the most **interesting** sound you ever **will** hear!

Make a list of other short-*i* words. Then use them in your cheer.

16

The Little Pink Pig

by Liza Charlesworth
illustrated by Doug Jones

■ SCHOLASTIC

Hip, Hip Hooray!

Kim was so **thrilled** to be a **little pink pig with** a **dimple in** her **chin** that she **did** a **big jig**! And **Kim** never **wished** to be **different** again.

14

I **wish** I looked **different**.

Kim did not like being **little** or **pink**. And she really **did** not like the **dimple in** her **chin**.

3

Once upon a time, there **lived** a **little pink pig**. Her name was **Kim**.

2

A

Short-i Riddles

Listen to the riddles. Then match each riddle with the right short-*i* word from the box.

Word Box				
jig	chicken	pig	wish	chimp
big	fish	grin	pink	mirror

1. This animal says, "Oink, oink!"
2. It means the opposite of *little*.
3. This bird lives on a farm and lays eggs.
4. Many pigs are this color.
5. This is another word for *monkey*.
6. You look in one to comb your hair.
7. This animal has fins and a tail.
8. This word means almost the same thing as *smile*.
9. A leprechaun does this kind of dance.
10. A fairy grants this with her magic wand.

Answers: 1. pig 2. big 3. chicken 4. pink 5. chimp 6. mirror 7. fish 8. grin 9. jig 10. wish

15

One day, **Kim** met a fairy named **Jill**. "I **will give** you **six wishes**," said Fairy **Jill**.

4

B

I missed this dimple!

"My **sixth wish is** to be me again," said **Kim with** a **grin**.
Zippity zip! Fairy **Jill did it**!

13

Then **Kim** remembered! She **still** had one **wish** left to **fix** her **mistake**.

"**Yippee!**" said **Kim**.
She **slipped** a **wish list** from her purse.

"My **fifth wish is** to have a cute **chin** like a **chimp**," said **Kim**.
Zippity zip! Fairy **Jill did it**!

"My second **wish is** to have green **skin** like a **lizard**," said **Kim**.
Zippity zip! Fairy **Jill did it**!

"My first **wish is** to be **big** like a **hippo**," said **Kim**.
Zippity zip! Fairy **Jill did it**!

6
C

Kim looked **in** the **silver mirror**.
"**Ick!** I'm so **mixed** up," cried **Kim**. "I **think** I **miss** the old me!"

11

"My third **wish is** to have **thick** feathers like a **chicken**," said **Kim**.
Zippity zip! Fairy **Jill did it**!

8
D

"My fourth **wish is** to have a **swishy** tail like a **fish**," said **Kim**.
Zippity zip! Fairy **Jill did it**!

9

Short-o Cheer

Hooray for short *o*, the best sound around!

Let's holler short-*o* words all over town!

There's **hog** and **tot** and **box** and **rock**.

There's **hop** and **fox** and **doll** and **lock**.

There's **chop** and **cot** and **mom** and **pop**.

There's **clock** and **job** and **pot** and **mop**.

Short *o*, short *o*, give a great cheer,

For the **jolliest** sound you ever will hear!

Make a list of other **short-*o*** words. Then use them in your cheer.

Phonics Tales!

short o

Todd's Odd Day

by Maria Fleming
illustrated by Kelly Kennedy

■ SCHOLASTIC

I am **fond** of **hotcakes**.

I like **hotcakes**, a **lot**, too!

OCTOPUS ESCAPES FROM AQUARIUM

APRICOT JAM

Or maybe **not**!

It is **hot**!

Yes, I'm **sopping** wet.

He saw a **hog** and a **dog** out for a **jog**.
"How **odd**!" said **Todd**.

One day, **Todd** went for a walk around the **block**. He saw **lots** of **odd** things.

2

A

I love hopscotch.

Yes, it's fun to **hop**.

He saw **ocelots** with **lots** of **spots**. "How **odd**!" said **Todd**.

4

B

Short-o Riddles

Listen to the riddles. Then match each riddle with the right short-*o* word from the box.

Word Box

jog	pot	mop	lollipop	socks
hog	top	hot	rock	tot

1. This is the opposite of *cold*.
2. You put these on your feet.
3. This is another word for *a young child*.
4. You do this when you run slowly.
5. This is another word for *pig*.
6. You can cook things in this.
7. This is the opposite of *bottom*.
8. This is another word for *stone*.
9. People use this to clean the floor.
10. This is a sweet treat that you lick.

Answers: 1. hot 2. socks 3. tot 4. jog 5. hog 6. pot 7. top 8. rock 9. mop 10. lollipop

15

Todd got dressed. He **trotted** down the stairs. **Todd's odd** day had just been an **odd** dream!

13

Suddenly, **Todd** heard a **knock**. He **popped** up in bed. "Wake up!" said his **mom**. **Todd** had been asleep!

He saw an **ostrich** dressed in **socks** with **dots**. "How **odd**!" said **Todd**.

Nice **shot**!

Nice **block**!

He saw **frogs** playing **soccer** in a parking **lot**. "How **odd**!" said **Todd**.

I will name my new **doll** Molly.

He saw a **crocodile** buy a **doll** for his **tot**. "How **odd**!" said **Todd**.

He saw a **lobster** leaving a **shop** with a **lollipop**.
"How **odd**!" said **Todd**.

6

C

He saw a **cop stop** an **otter on** a **log**.
"How **odd**!" said **Todd**.

11

He saw a **fox bebop** with a **mop**.
"How **odd**!" said **Todd**.

8

D

He saw an **ox** mail a **box** of **rocks**. "How **odd**!"
said **Todd**.

9

Short-u Cheer

Hooray for short *u*, the best sound around!

Let's holler short-*u* words all over town!

There's **mug** and **sun** and **lunch** and **up**.

There's **gum** and **fun** and **luck** and **cup**.

There's **bug** and **hut** and **hum** and **rug**.

There's **lump** and **run** and **chum** and **hug**.

Short *u*, short *u*, give a great cheer,

For the **luckiest** sound you ever will hear!

Make a list of other short-*u* words. Then use them in your cheer.

Phonics Tales!

short u

Lucky Duck

by Teddy Slater
illustrated by Kellie Lewis

SCHOLASTIC

Yum! It was **just** what he wanted. Oh, what a **lucky duck**!

Duck rushed downstairs. He was **hungry** for **plum** pancakes with plenty of **butter** and **syrup**.

Phonics Fact
Sometimes the short-*u* sound comes in the second syllable of a word, such as in sy**rup**.

One **sunny Sunday**, **Duck** woke **up** in **such** a great mood. He had a **hunch** this would be his **lucky** day.

Duck opened the **cupboard**. Uh-oh! No **plums**.

Short-u Riddles

Listen to the riddles. Then match each riddle with the right short-*u* word from the box.

Word Box

yum	duck	snug	luck	up
jump	plum	Sunday	butter	summer

1. This animal says, "Quack, quack."
2. You put this on toast or popcorn.
3. This is the day after Saturday.
4. It is the opposite of *down*.
5. This word rhymes with *rug*.
6. A four-leaf clover brings this.
7. It means almost the same thing as *leap*.
8. This is the season after spring.
9. You say this when something is delicious.
10. This purple fruit is bigger than a grape.

Answers: 1. duck 2. butter 3. Sunday 4. up 5. snug 6. luck 7. jump 8. summer 9. yum 10. plum

Duck rushed off to the **Snug** Diner and placed his order: a stack of **plum** pancakes with plenty of **butter** and **syrup**.

Gus gave Duck a hug and a coupon for a free brunch at the Snug Diner on Huff Street.

So Duck jumped in his truck and headed to Gus's Store to get some plums. But the truck hit a bump and would not budge.

Duck had never felt less lucky. Then, uh-oh! He dropped his plums.

"I will just have to walk," said Duck. But along the way, he got stuck in bubble gum. Ugh!

When **Duck** got out of his **truck**—yuck!
He stepped in a big **puddle** of **mud**.

6

C

But suddenly... **Duck** heard a **drum** roll.
Then **Gus** said, "Congratulations! You are the
one **hundredth customer** of the **summer**."

11

Still, **Duck trudged** on. That is, **until** he got
stung on the **thumb** by a **bumblebee**.
What an **ugly lump**!

8

D

By the time **Duck** got to **Gus's** Store,
his **tummy** was **rumbling**. He was very
hungry, **plus** very **grumpy**.

9

Long-a Cheer

Hooray for long *a*, the best sound around!

Let's holler long-*a* words all over town!

There's **ape** and **date** and **jay** and **snake**.

There's **brave** and **grape** and **bake** and **cake**.

There's **day** and **say** and **stain** and **quaint**.

There's **great** and **break** and **chain** and **paint**.

Long *a*, long *a*, give **a great** cheer

For the most **amazing** sound you'll ever hear!

> Make a list of other long-*a* words. Then use them in your cheer.

16

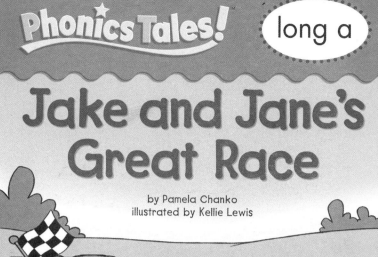

Phonics Tales! long a

Jake and Jane's Great Race

by Pamela Chanko
illustrated by Kellie Lewis

■SCHOLASTIC

"But I'm in such **amazing shape**!"

But it was **way** too **late**. **Jane** won first **place**!
"You did **great**! Want to **make a statement**?" asked **Abe**.
"Slow and steady wins the **race**," said **Jane**.

14

"Okay!"

"No **way**!"

"No **way**!" said **Abe**.
But **Jane** said, "**Okay**! Let's **race today**!"
That **Jane** sure was **brave**!

> **Phonics Fact**
> The long-*a* sound can also be made by the letters *ay*, as in **way** and **okay**. Can you find another word on this page that uses *ay* to stand for long *a*?
> (Answer: **today**)

3

Jake Snake was in super **shape**. So **Jake** challenged his friends **Jane** and **Abe** to **race** around **Drake Lake**.

2

A

Long-a Riddles

Listen to the riddles. Then match each riddle with the right long-*a* word from the box.

Word Box				
snake	paint	day	late	brave
cake	Jake	grapes	plate	race

1. It is the opposite of *early*.
2. It is the opposite of *fearful*.
3. You dip a brush in this to make a picture.
4. Your birthday candles go on top of this.
5. This animal slithers and makes a hissing sound.
6. This fruit comes in a bunch.
7. This boy's name rhymes with *bake*.
8. You can run in this kind of contest.
9. This is round and you put food on it.
10. It is the opposite of *night*.

Answers: 1. late 2. brave 3. paint 4. cake 5. snake 6. grapes 7. Jake 8. race 9. plate 10. day

15

Everyone **came** to see the **race**.
"I'm so **amazing**! I can't **wait** to win!" boasted **Jake**.
"You **may** be surprised!" replied **Jane**.

4

B

But **Jake** took **a break** and **ate a** big **plate** of **grapes**!
Then he heard **Abe say**, "**Hey, Jane** is winning!"
That **made Jake** decide to join the **race**.

13

Hey, Jane is winning!

Jane **raced** and **raced**.

The two **racers** took their **places**.
"Ready, set, go!" yelled **Abe**.

Jane **raced** and **raced**.

But **Jake** took **a break** to **bake a layer** cake.

Phonics Fact
The long-*a* sound is sometimes made with an *ea*, as in **break** and **great**. And guess what? A stand-alone *a* can make the long-*a* sound, too!

Jane raced and raced.

C

But **Jake** took **a break** to call his friend **named Dave**, who lived in **Spain**.

Jane raced and raced.

D

But **Jake** took **a break** to **make a quaint painting** of Drake Lake.

Long-e Cheer

Hooray for long *e*, the best sound around!

Let's holler long-*e* words all over town!

There's **queen** and **bee** and **cheese** and **scream**.

There's **clean** and **read** and **tea** and **dream**.

There's **me** and **we** and **she** and **he**.

There's **brief** and **chief** and **deep** and **sea**.

Long *e*, long *e*, give a great cheer

For the **neatest** sound you ever will hear!

Make a list of other **long-*e*** words. Then use them in your cheer.

16

Queen Bee's Scream

by Liza Charlesworth
illustrated by Patrick Girouard

SCHOLASTIC

YES, **INDEED**!

"YES, **INDEED!**" screamed the **bees**.
"**We** love you, **Queen Bee**!"

14

I **NEED** YOUR HELP TODAY, **BEES**!

Phonics Fact
The vowel pair *ea* can also make the long-*e* sound, as in **mean**. Can you find another word on this page that uses *ea* to stand for the long-*e* sound?
(Answer: **screamed**)

Everyone thought **Queen Bee** was **mean** because she screamed.

3

Meet Queen Bee.

A

Long-e Riddles

Listen to the riddles. Then match each riddle with the right long-*e* word from the box.

Word Box

queen	sweet	flea	bee	mean
clean	scream	leaves	sweep	bean

1 This bug has black and yellow stripes.

2 A princess grows up to be this.

3 It is the opposite of *dirty*.

4 You do this with a broom.

5 It is the opposite of *sour*.

6 It is the opposite of *nice*.

7 These grow on the branches of trees.

8 It means almost the same thing as *yell*.

9 This vegetable rhymes with *mean*.

10 This bug sometimes makes dogs itch.

Answers: 1. bee 2. queen 3. clean 4. sweep 5. sweet 6. mean 7. leaves 8. scream 9. bean 10. flea

Phonics Fact

The long-*e* sound can be made with a single *e*, too. Words that follow this spelling pattern include **she**, **he**, **me**, and **be**.

"**Feed** our pet **flea**!" **she screamed** at **Jean Bee**. But **Jean Bee** buzzed away.

B

"**My sweet bees**, I am **really** sorry that I **screamed** and did not say **please**," said **Queen Bee** softly. "Can you **each** forgive **me**?"

"That is **easy**," said **Queen Bee**. "**Please** go tell the **bees** to **meet me beneath** the **tree** for a **speech**."
"I will **be** back **before** you can count to **three**," squeaked Benny Bee.

SWEEP UP THESE LEAVES!

"**Sweep** up **these leaves!**" she screamed at **Lee Bee**.
But **Lee Bee** buzzed away.

"I **see**," said **Queen Bee**. "I was just using my outdoor voice so all the **bees** could hear **me**. From now on, I will **speak softly**."

Beehive

CLEAN OUR HIVE UNTIL IT GLEAMS!

"**Clean** our hive until it **gleams!**" she screamed at **Dee Bee**.
But **Dee Bee** buzzed away.

"**Weed** the **bean** garden!" **she screamed** at **Sheena Bee**.
But **Sheena Bee** buzzed away.

6   C

"**Neat**!" **squeaked Benny Bee**. "And there's one more thing: "When you **need** our help, would you say **please**?"

11

Phonics Fact
When a word ends in *y*, the *y* sometimes makes a long-*e* sound, as in **Benny**. Can you find another word on this page that uses a *y* to stand for the long-*e* sound?
(Answer: **majesty**)

"Make some **peach tea**!" **she screamed** at **Benny Bee**.
But **Benny Bee** DID NOT **flee**. **He** just made her **majesty** some **tea**.

8   D

Phonics Fact
The long-*e* sound is sometimes made by the vowel pair *ie*, as in **believe**. Other long-*e* words with this spelling pattern include **chief** and **niece**.

"**Benny**, I **need** to ask you something!" **screamed Queen Bee**. "Why do all the **bees speed** away when I **speak**?"
"I **believe** the **reason** is that you **scream**," **squeaked Benny Bee**.

9

Long-i Cheer

Hooray for long *i*, the best sound around!

Let's holler long-*i* words all over town!

There's **like** and **nice** and **bike** and **kite**.

There's **fly** and **sky** and **light** and **night**.

There's **pie** and **my** and **five** and **find**.

There's **write** and **rice** and **size** and **kind**.

Long *i*, long *i*, give a great cheer

For the **finest** sound you ever will hear!

Make a list of other long-*i* words. Then use them in your cheer.

Phonics Tales!   long i

Ike and Mike

by Maria Fleming
illustrated by Kelly Kennedy

SCHOLASTIC

The **fly smiles** with **delight** as he turns out the **light**. "What a **sight**! Sleep **tight**! Good **night**!"

Ike does not **like** to share with **Mike**.
Mike does not **like** to share with **Ike**.

Phonics Fact
This book is full of long-*i* words. Many times this sound is made by a silent *e*. The vowel *i* is followed by a consonant, which is then followed by a silent *e*, as in **Ike** and **Mike**. What other long-*i* words can you find in this story? Look at the pictures, too!

This is **Ike**. This is **Ike's** brother, **Mike**.

A

Long-i Riddles

Listen to the riddles. Then match each riddle with the right long-*i* word from the box.

Word Box				
fly	dime	bite	smile	pie
hi	wise	lime	bike	night

1. You do this when you are happy.
2. This is something you eat for dessert.
3. You can buy things with this coin.
4. This is a bug.
5. This has wheels and you can ride it.
6. It means *smart*.
7. It is the opposite of *day*.
8. This green fruit tastes sour.
9. It means the same thing as *hello*.
10. You do this when you eat an apple.

Answers: 1. smile 2. pie 3. dime 4. fly 5. bike 6. wise 7. night 8. lime 9. hi 10. bite

Phonics Fact
The long-*i* sound can also be made with a single *i* as in **I**. Another word with this spelling pattern is **hi**.

Ike has a new **white bike**.
"Can **I ride** your **bike**?" **Mike** asks **Ike**.
"No way!" says **Ike**. "It's **mine**!"

B

That **night**, **Ike** shares his book of **rhymes** with **Mike**. **Mike** shares his stuffed **lion**, **Spike**, with **Ike**.

Ike and Mike think sharing is **mighty fine**!

Phonics Fact

Sometimes the letter *y* makes the long-*i* sound, as in **fly** and **sky**. Can you find two other words on this page with *y* that make the long-*i* sound?

(Answer: **try, my**)

Mike likes to **fly** his **kite** in the **sky**.
"Can **I try** to **fly** your **kite**?" **Ike** asks **Mike**.
"No way!" says **Mike**. "It's **mine**!"

Then **Ike** and **Mike** begin to **cry**. A **wise fly** buzzes **by**.
"Boys, take **my advice**," he says with a **sigh**.
"It's **nice** to share."

"No way!" says **Ike**. "It's **mine**! Can **I try** a **bite** of **pie**?"
"No way!" says **Mike**. "It's **mine**!"

Phonics Fact

The vowel pair *ie* can also make the long-*i* sound, as in **fries**. Can you find another long-*i* word with the same spelling pattern on this page?

(Answer: **pie**)

At **lunchtime**, **Ike** has French **fries**. **Mike** has **lime pie**.
"Can **I try** a **fry**?" **Mike** asks **Ike**.

6   C

"That **fly might** just be **right**," says **Ike**.
"Let's give it a **try**," says **Mike**.

11

Ike and **Mike spy** a toy. They each have **five dimes**. Will they share their **dimes** to get the toy? No way!

8   D

Phonics Fact

Another spelling pattern that makes the long-*i* sound is *igh*, as in **fight**. Other words with this pattern are **sigh**, **might**, and **right**. Be on the lookout for more!

Ike and **Mike** begin to **fight**.

9

Long-o Cheer

Hooray for long *o*, the best sound around!

Let's holler long-*o* words all over town!

There's **mole** and **hole** and **phone** and **rose**.

There's **toad** and **road** and **home** and **hose**.

There's **snow** and **grow** and **no** and **go**.

There's **cold** and **gold** and **hoe** and **toe**.

Long *o*, long *o*, give a great cheer,

For the **boldest** sound you ever will hear!

Make a list of other **long-*o*** words. Then use them in your cheer.

16

At Home With Mole and Toad

by Maria Fleming
illustrated by Doug Jones

SCHOLASTIC

Stroll, stroll, stroll along.
Stroll right down the road.
I'm a mole who likes to stroll.
I'm off to visit Toad!

No! This time, **Mole** will **stroll**!

14

Phonics Fact

The vowel pair *oa* can also make the long-*o* sound, as in **toad** and **road**. Can you find two words in the picture that use *oa* to stand for the long-*o* sound?

(Answer: **goat**, **boat**)

One day, **Toad phones Mole**.

3

Phonics Fact

This book is full of long-*o* words. Many times this sound is made by a silent *e*. The vowel *o* is followed by a consonant, which is then followed by a silent *e*, as in **mole** and **hole**. What other long-*o* words can you find in this story? Look at the pictures, too!

Mole lives in a **hole**. Her friend **Toad** lives down the **road**.

2

A

Long-o Riddles

Listen to the riddles. Then match each riddle with the right long-*o* word from the box.

Word Box

toad	toes	phone	cold	go
road	mole	toast	rose	snow

1. This is white and falls from the sky.
2. This small, furry animal lives in a hole.
3. It is the opposite of *stop*.
4. It means the same as *street*.
5. This tastes good with butter on it.
6. You have five of these on each foot.
7. It is a kind of flower.
8. You use it to talk to someone.
9. This animal is a lot like a frog.
10. It is the opposite of *hot*.

Answers: 1. snow 2. mole 3. go 4. road 5. toast 6. toes 7. rose 8. phone 9. toad 10. cold

15

Phonics Fact

A single *o* can also make the long-*o* sound, as in **over** and **okay**. Try to spot other words that use one *o* to make the long-*o* sound.

"**Won't** you come **over** for **toast** and **cocoa**," asks **Toad**.
"**Okay**!" says **Mole**.

4

B

Toad invites **Mole over** for **oatmeal** cookies and **cold** milk. How will **Mole go** down the **road** to **Toad's**? Will **Mole roll**?

13

"That is **okay**," says **Toad**. "I **know** you did not mean to **roll over** everything. I **know** you did not mean to hurt **Joe** or my **toe**."

Mole wants to **show Toad** her new **yellow** skates. So she puts them on and **rolls** down the **road**.

Mole rolls home, feeling **low**.

Mole rolls into **Toad's home**. She **rolls** into a table and knocks **over** the **cocoa** and **toast**.

Mole **rolls** down a **slope**. She **rolls over** a **hose**.
Then **Mole rolls over** the **roses Toad grows**.

C

The next day, **Mole phones Toad.**
"I am **so, so, so, so, so, SO** sorry," says **Mole.**

Phonics Fact

The vowel pair oe—as in **Joe**—can make the long-o sound, too. Can you find a long-o word with this spelling pattern on page 9?

(Answer: **toe**)

Mole **rolls** into a shelf. She knocks **over Toad's** snow globes. She spills the **bowl** that **holds** Mole's goldfish, Joe.

D

Mole even **rolls** right **over Toad's toe**! Toad **moans** and **groans**. He **scolds Mole**, "**No** more **rolling**! Mole, you must **go**!"

Long-u Cheer

Hooray for long *u*, the best sound around!

Let's holler long-*u* words all over town!

There's **cube** and **cute** and **huge** and **mule**.

There's **music** and **bugle** and **menu** and **fuel**.

There's **fuse** and **fume** and **youth** and **few**.

There's **uniform**, **cucumber**, **perfume**, and **you**.

Long *u*, long *u*, give a great cheer,

For the most **useful** sound **you** ever will hear!

Make a list of other **long-***u* words. Then use them in your cheer.

16

Phonics Tales!

A Mule Named Sugar Cube

by Maria Fleming
illustrated by Margeaux Lucas

SCHOLASTIC

Hooray for Sugar **Cube**, the **cutest mule** in the **universe**!

But she is still very **cute**!

14

I'll have a **huge** bowl of sugar **cubes**.

HUGO'S DINER MENU

Phonics Fact

The letter *u* does not always need the help of silent *e* to make the long-*u* sound. Sometimes a single *u* makes the sound all by itself. The word **unusual** has two long-*u* sounds in it! Can you find two words in the picture that use a single *u* to make the long-*u* sound?

(Answer: **Hugo's, menu**)

Sugar **Cube** is not like other **mules**.
Sugar **Cube** is **unusual**.

3

Phonics Fact

This book is full of long-*u* words. Many times this sound is made by a silent *e*. The vowel *u* is followed by a consonant, which is then followed by a silent *e*, as in **cube** and **mule**. What other long-*u* words can you find in this story? Look at the pictures, too!

This is Sugar **Cube**. Sugar **Cube** is a very **cute mule**.

2

A

Long-u Riddles

Listen to the riddles. Then match each riddle with the right long-*u* word from the box.

Word Box

cube	music	few	museum	menu
mule	huge	you	cute	computer

1. This farm animal looks kind of like a horse.
2. It is the opposite of *me*.
3. You use this to order food at a restaurant.
4. It means *very big*.
5. You can use this to write, play games, or send e-mail.
6. You can see art in this building.
7. This has a square shape.
8. It rhymes with *flute*.
9. It is the opposite of *many*.
10. You hear this on the radio.

Answers: 1. mule 2. you 3. menu 4. huge 5. computer 6. museum 7. cube 8. cute 9. few 10. music

15

Sugar **Cube** can **use** a **computer**.

4

B

Sugar **Cube** even takes the other **mules** to the **museum**. Now Sugar **Cube** is not such an **unusual mule**.

13

Sugar **Cube** teaches the other **mules** how to **use** a **computer**. She teaches them how to ride a **unicycle** and play the **bugle**.

Sugar **Cube** loves **music**. She can play the **bugle**.

Sugar **Cube** tries to do **regular mule** things. But it's no **use**. **Regular mule** things do not **amuse** her.

Sugar **Cube** can ride a **unicycle**.

Sugar **Cube** likes to go to the **museum**.

C

Then Sugar **Cube** gets a **useful** idea.

Phonics Fact

The letters *ew* sometimes make the long-*u* sound, as in **few**. The letters *you* also make the long-*u* sound, as in **youthful**. Can you find other long-*u* words on this page that use these spelling patterns?

(Answer: mew, Matthew, you)

One day, a **few youthful mules** call Sugar **Cube** over.

"**Excuse** me," says a **mule** named **Matthew**.

"But **you** should act like a **regular mule**."

D

Matthew hurt Sugar **Cube's** feelings. Sugar **Cube** wants to fit in. She wants to be part of the **mule community**.

OO Cheer

Hooray for o-o, the best pair around!

Let's holler o-o words all over town!

There's **school** and **choose** and **roof** and **moon**.

There's **gloom** and **room** and **scoop** and **soon**.

There's **bloom** and **toot** and **tool** and **noodle**.

There's **boot** and **scoot** and **zoo** and **poodle**.

O-o, o-o, give a great cheer,

For the **grooviest** sound you ever will hear!

> Make a list of other *oo* words that make the same sound as these. Then use them in your cheer.

Goo, Goo!

by Teddy Slater
illustrated by Cary Pillo

SCHOLASTIC

That's the **cool** thing about the kid. I love him and he loves me, **too**! If I could pick any brother, I would always **choose** him!

But all my brother says is, "**Goo, goo!**" He is **too** little to talk. He just opens up his **googly** eyes. Then he smiles his **goofy** grin and **drools**.

> Goo, goo!

Ooh!

Kitchy, kitchy **coo**!

Phonics Fact

The story you are about to read is full of *oo* words. This pair of vowels is called a digraph. That means the two vowels work together to make a single sound, as in the words **too**, **ooh**, and **goo**, **goo**. What other *oo* words can you find in this story? Look at the pictures, too!

Everyone thinks my brother is **too** cute for words. "Kitchy, kitchy, **coo**!" they say. "**Ooh**, he is so sweet!" they **croon**.

2

A

---

section header

OO Riddles

Listen to the riddles. Then match each riddle with the right *oo* word from the box.

Word Box

soon	toot	moose	moon	school
moo	boom	poodle	kangaroo	afternoon

1 What a cow says.

2 This animal hops and has a pouch.

3 This is the sound that a train makes.

4 You go to this place to learn.

5 Fireworks make this sound.

6 It means *in a little while*.

7 This animal has big antlers.

8 You can see this in the night sky along with stars.

9 This kind of dog has curly hair.

10 It is the time between morning and night.

Answers: 1. moo 2. kangaroo 3. toot 4. school 5. boom 6. soon 7. moose 8. moon 9. poodle 10. afternoon

15

Hoot!

Moo!

Phonics Fact

Sometimes the *oo* sound appears in the second syllable of a word, as in **raccoon** and **baboon**. Can you find a word on this page with the *oo* sound in the third syllable?

(Answer: **kangaroo**)

My brother's **room** is like a **zoo**. He has a **moose**, a **goose**, a **raccoon**, a **poodle**, a **baboon**, and a big **kangaroo**.

4

B

Smooch!

Goo, goo!

I **scoot** over to his crib, **scoop** him up, and give him a big **smooch**. And just like that, he goes from "**Boo, hoo**!" to "**Goo, goo**!"

13

If he is not in the **mood** to sleep, my brother cries, "**Boo**, **hoo**! **Boo**, **hoo**!" My parents try **oodles** of things to make him stop. But I'm the only one who can.

He has an owl that says, "**Hoot**!" and a cow that says, "**Moo**!" Everyone gives him stuffed animals.

Phonics Fact

Sometimes *oo* is pronounced differently than in the words **too**, **ooh**, and **goo**, **goo**. It can also make the sound found in *good*, *wood*, and *took*. Can you find a word on page 11 with the same *oo* sound as in *good*?

(Answer: **books**)

But as **soon** as I come home from **school**, he wakes up. Then he gives me that good old grin and we play and play!

My brother likes my toys, **too**. I have a car that goes **VROOM** and a plane that goes **ZOOM**. I have a drum that goes **BOOM! BOOM! BOOM!** And I have a **choo-choo** train with a red **caboose**.

But does my brother say thanks? Nope.
He just says, "**Goo, goo!**" That is all he can say:
"**Goo, goo! Goo, goo!**"

C

At night, in the **moonlight**, I help Mom put on
his **booties**. She reads him fun books like *Winnie
the Pooh.* After that, I **toot** my **kazoo** and sing,
"Yankee **Doodle** Dandy."

My brother has just one **tooth** so he only eats
gooey foods. "**Goo, goo!**" he says when you
give him a **noodle.** He can't even use a **spoon!**

D

After lunch, his eyes get **droopy**. Sometimes he
even **snoozes** all **afternoon.**

OU Cheer

Hooray for *o-u*, the best pair around!

Let's holler *o-u* words all over town!

There's **house** and **mouse** and **scout** and **found**.

There's **out** and **pout** and **round** and **ground**.

There's **count** and **south** and **mouth** and **cloud**.

There's **bounce** and **ounce** and **trout** and **proud**.

O-u, o-u, give a great cheer,

For the **loudest sound** you ever will hear!

Make a list of other *ou* words. Then use them in your cheer.

16

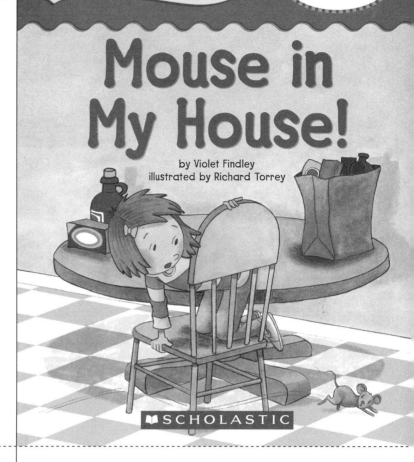

Phonics Tales!

ou

Mouse in My House!

by Violet Findley
illustrated by Richard Torrey

■SCHOLASTIC

And that **mouse** never bothers me an **ounce**. Except when he **devours** my **Sour** Gummy Worms!

14

EEEEEEEK!

Phonics Fact

Sometimes the *ou* sound appears in the second syllable of a word, as in **around**. Be on the lookout for more *ou* words like this!

When I looked **around**, I saw a **mouse** on the **counter**.
"EEEEEEEK!" I **shouted**. "Out of my **house**, Mouse!"

3

Squeak! Squeak!

Phonics Fact
The story you are about to read is full of *ou* words. This pair of vowels is called a diphthong. That means the *o* and the *u* work together to make a smooth sound that glides from one vowel sound to the next, as in the words **found**, **mouse**, and **loud**. What other *ou* words can you find in this story? Look at the pictures, too!

This is a story **about** the day I **found** a **mouse** in my **house**. It all started with a **loud** squeaking **sound**.

2   A

OUCH!

But that **mouse bounded** onto the **ground** and **bounced** off my shoe. "OUCH!" I **shouted**.

4   B

Listen to the riddles. Then match each riddle with the right *ou* word from the box.

Word Box

loud	sour	mouse	mouth	out
house	shout	found	hour	mountain

1. This tiny, furry animal loves cheese.
2. It is the opposite of *quiet*.
3. Lemons taste this way.
4. Another word for a *home*.
5. It is the same amount of time as 60 minutes.
6. It is the opposite of *lost*.
7. This means almost the same thing as *yell*.
8. You use this part of your body to eat and talk.
9. It is the opposite of *in*.
10. This is the word for a *very, very tall hill*.

Answers: 1. mouse 2. loud 3. sour 4. house 5. hour 6. found 7. shout 8. mouth 9. out 10. mountain

15

I am **proud** to say that the **mouse** and I are now pals. In fact, he lives with me in my **house**.

13

"I'm sorry I was a **grouch**," I said **loudly**.
Then that **mouse bounded** onto my hand.
"Squeak, squeak!" went his tiny **mouth**.

Next, the **mouse** knocked over a five-**pound**
bag of **flour**. Then, he scurried **about**, leaving
clouds of **flour** all **around**!

And guess who was **lounging** beside me?
The **mouse**!

"**Out** of my **house, Mouse!**" I **shouted**.
But the **mouse bounded** onto a **round** table.
He **pounced** on my **Sour** Gummy Worms and
ate **about** a **thousand**! (I **counted**.)

"Out of my **house, Mouse!**" I **shouted**.
But that **mouse bounded** onto a **mountain**
of clothes and curled up on my best **blouse**!

6

C

When I looked at the **mouse**, he was
trembling. Why, that **mouse** was not **lousy**
at all! He was just scared.

11

Then, that **lousy mouse bounded out** of the
room. I was **outraged**! Where did he go?
I **scouted around** for **hours**.

8

D

Well, I never **found** that **mouse**, so I plopped
on the **couch** to **pout**.

9

Silent-e Cheer

Hooray for silent *e* and its long-vowel sound!

Let's holler silent-e words all over town!

There's **Pete** and **like, concrete** and **slide**.

There's **robe** and **cone** and **bike** and **hide**.

There's **cute** and **cube** and **mule** and **name**.

There's **joke** and **rope** and **cake** and **game**.

Silent *e*! Silent *e*! Let's cheer for a **while**,

For words that always **make** us **smile**!

> Make a list of other silent-*e* words. Then use them in your cheer.

Phonics Tales!   silent e

Porcupine Pete

by Maria Fleming
illustrated by Steve Björkman

■ SCHOLASTIC

Pete, I would not **trade** you for anything in the **whole wide** world.

Me, neither.

Pete is always by my **side**. **Life** would not be **complete** without my pet, **Pete**!

Do you want to get an **ice** cream **cone**?

Nope. I need to get **home**.

These are my other friends **Dave, Mike,** and **Eve**.

Phonics Fact

The words **these**, **Rose**, **Luke**, **Jane**, and **Steve** are all silent-*e* words because you don't hear the *e* at the end of the word. But the silent *e* still has a job to do. It makes the vowel sound in these words a long-vowel sound. What other silent-*e* words can you find in this story? Look at the pictures, too!

My name is **Rose**. **These** are my friends **Luke**, **Jane**, and **Steve**.

2

A

Phonics Fact

Look at the words **pet** and **Pete**. By putting a silent *e* at the end of *pet*, the vowel sound changes from short *e* to long *e*. It makes a new word. Be on the lookout for more silent-*e* words with the long-*e* sound.

They are good friends. But my very best friend is my pet, **Pete**. **Pete** and I do everything together.

4

B

Silent-e Riddles

Listen to the riddles. Then match each riddle with the silent-*e* word from the box.

Word Box				
slide	Pete	nose	cake	huge
wide	cape	cute	rose	lake

1. This is a kind of flower.
2. People use this word to describe babies.
3. Superman wears one of these.
4. This is a great place to go fishing.
5. It is a boy's name.
6. You use this to smell.
7. It is the opposite of *narrow*.
8. You eat this sweet treat on your birthday.
9. This means *very big*.
10. You find this at a playground.

Answers: 1. rose 2. cute 3. cape 4. lake 5. Pete 6. nose 7. wide 8. cake 9. huge 10. slide

15

We just **use** marshmallows!

13

It can be tricky to give **Pete** a hug. But it's not a **huge** problem.

Pete is a great **athlete**. We love to **compete**.

Sometimes we dress in a cap and **cape**. We pretend we are **brave** superheroes.

We **like** to sit **side**-by-**side** on a double-**wide** **slide**. Down we **glide**!

Phonics Fact

Look at the words **spin** and **spine**. By putting a silent *e* at the end of *spin*, the vowel sound changes from short *i* to long *i*. It makes a new word. Be on the lookout for more silent-*e* words with the long-*i* sound.

I spin **Pete** on the merry-go-round. It tickles his **spines**.

C

Pete and I **make fake cakes** for picnics by the **lake**.

Phonics Fact

Look at the words **hop** and **hope**. By putting a silent *e* at the end of *hop*, the vowel sound changes from short *o* to long *o*. It makes a new word. Be on the lookout for more silent-*e* words with the long-*o* sound.

Pete and I play hopscotch together. I **hope** to hop as well as **Pete** one day.

D

We love to **pose** in silly **clothes**. In a **robe**, I'm a queen on a **throne**. **Pete's** a clown in a **cone** hat and funny **nose**.

Bossy-r Cheer

Hooray for bossy *r*, the best sound around!

Let's shout bossy-*r* words all over town!

There's **fur** and **fern** and **fork** and **car**.

There's **shirt** and **turn** and **her** and **star**.

There's **start** and **stork** and **barn** and **corn**.

There's **surf** and **herd** and **porch** and **horn**.

Bossy *r*, bossy *r*, give a great cheer

For the **sharpest** sound you ever will hear!

Make a list of other bossy-*r* words. Then use them in your cheer.

Bert's Super Circus

by Liza Charlesworth
illustrated by Stephen Gilpin

SCHOLASTIC

Phonics Fact

Bird, **turtle**, **serpent**, **stork**, and **shark** are all bossy-*r* words. Remember: When you see an *r* right after a vowel, that *r* usually takes charge and changes the vowel's sound.

Wow! **Bert's Super Circus** has come to an end.
The **performers** do hope you will all come again!

Boys and **girls** of any age,
to **start** the show, just **turn** the page!

Bert's Super Circus

Phonics Fact

Bert, circus, start, and turn are all bossy-r words. In bossy-r words, the r takes charge and changes the sound of the vowel it immediately follows. Say bet and Bert. Bet makes a short-e sound. But when r is added, as in Bert, the e makes a very different sound. Can you find more bossy-r words in this story? Look at the pictures, too!

Step right up, **gather** round!
Bert's Super Circus is in town!

A

Bossy-r Riddles

Listen to the riddles. Then match each riddle with the right bossy-r word from the box.

Word Box				
stars	fern	large	fork	circle
bird	turtle	circus	serpent	purple

1 This animal flies and chirps.

2 This goes along with a spoon and knife.

3 It is a kind of plant.

4 These shine in the night sky.

5 It is the name for a round shape.

6 This animal is a lot like a tortoise.

7 It is a kind of snake.

8 Some grapes are this color.

9 Clowns, animals, and jugglers are part of this show.

10 It is the opposite of small.

Answers: 1. bird 2. fork 3. fern 4. stars 5. circle 6. turtle 7. serpent 8. purple 9. circus 10. large

---

First, a **bird** named **Shirley** will **chirp** "Happy **Birthday**"

B

then strum a **harp** atop a **large** cookie **jar**! What a **star**!

Phonics Fact

Charming and shark are both -ar words. What others do you see on this page?

Last, a **charming shark** named **Marla** will play **guitar** in a **car**

Chirp, chirp, chirp!

as she **whirls** and **twirls** a baton in a **circle**.

Phonics Fact
First and bird are both -ir words. What others do you see on this page?

Then, a **stork** named **Mort** will play an **enormous horn**

Hurrah!

and pull out a **furry purple** rabbit with a **curly** tail!

Phonics Fact
Turtle and Kurt are both -ur words. What others do you see on this page?

Then, a **turtle** named **Kurt** will reach into a magic **urn**

C

Popcorn! Popcorn!

and use **forty forks** to **form** an amazing **fort**.

Phonics Fact
Stork and **Norm** are both *-or* words. What others do you see on this page?

Then, a **serpent** named **Fern** will **enter** a **silver** door

D

Terrific!

and **emerge perched** on **her** favorite **dessert**!

Phonics Fact
Serpent and **Fern** are both *-er* words. What others do you see on this page?

ST Cheer

Hooray for *s-t*, the best sound around!

Let's holler *s-t* words all over town!

There's **stop** and **stuff** and **storm** and **pest**.

There's **stilts** and **stunts** and **stairs** and **best**.

There's **sister**, **monster**, **still**, and **fast**.

There's **star** and **sticky**, **first**, and **last**.

S-t, *s-t*, give a great cheer,

For the **most stylish** sound you ever will hear!

> Make a list of other *st* words. Then use them in your cheer.

Phonics Tales!

st

Stan the Pest

by Pamela Chanko
illustrated by Amy Wummer

SCHOLASTIC

Stan did all his **funniest stunts** for **Stacy**. He didn't **stop** until the **storm** was over. "**Stan**, you may be a **pest**," **Stacy** said. "But you're also the **best** brother ever!"

Stacy was **Stan's** big **sister**. She **just** thought **Stan** was a **pest**.

Stan was a boy who **just** loved to get attention. He could never sit **still**.

A

Every day, **Stan** tried a new **stunt**. **First**, he **stood** on his head.

B

ST Riddles

Listen to the riddles. Then match each riddle with the right *st* word from the box. (Hint: Sometimes the *st* appears in the middle or at the end of the word.)

Word Box				
stop	stairs	pest	monster	fast
stilts	sister	storm	best	star

1. It is the opposite of *brother*.
2. This kind of weather might have rain or snow.
3. It is the opposite of *go*.
4. You can walk on these to look taller.
5. If you see one in the night sky, you can make a wish on it.
6. It is a scary make-believe creature.
7. You can walk up them or down them.
8. This word means the opposite of *worst*.
9. You move this way when you run quickly.
10. This word describes someone who bothers you.

Answers: 1. sister 2. storm 3. stop 4. stilts 5. star 6. monster 7. stairs 8. best 9. fast 10. pest

---

That night, there was a big **storm**. When **Stacy** heard the thunder **start**, she was scared to be alone.

"**Stan**! Come here **fast**!" she called.

At **last**, **Stan** **stopped**.
"A **pest**! **Stacy must** not want me around," he thought.
So **Stan** went up the **stairs** to his own room.

But **Stacy just** said, "**Stop** it, **Stan**."

Next, **Stan** made a **stage** from a **stack** of books and pretended to be the **greatest** rock **star** ever.

But **Stacy just** said, "**Stop** it, **Stan**."

Next, **Stan** tried walking on **stilts**.

6

But **Stacy just** said, "**Stop** it, **Stan**. You are such a **pest**!"

11

Phonics Fact

Sometimes the *st* sound comes in the middle of a word, as in **monster** and **sister**.

Next, **Stan** put **sticky stuff** in his hair and pretended to be a **monster**.

8

But **Stacy just** said, "**Stop** it, **Stan**."

9

SK Cheer

Hooray for s-k, the best sound around!

Let's holler s-k words all over town!

There's **skunk** and **skip** and **skit** and **mask**.

There's **skin** and **sketch** and **desk** and **task**.

There's **skate** and **sky** and **skill** and **dusk**.

There's **skirt** and **skull** and **ski** and **tusk**.

S-k, s-k, shout hip-hip-hooray,

For a sound that takes great **skill** to say!

> Make a list of other *sk* words. Then use them in your cheer.

16

Skippy Skunk

by Maria Fleming
illustrated by Jackie Snider

■ SCHOLASTIC

So **Skippy Skunk** took **Skylar skydiving**. Now they both have a brand-new **skill**. And a brand-new friend!

14

Skippy Skunk can make **masks**. **Skippy Skunk** can do **skits**.

> **Phonics Fact**
>
> Sometimes the *sk* blend comes at the end of a word, as in **mask**. Can you find another word on this page that ends in the *sk* blend? Be on the lookout for more!
>
> (Answer: **desk**)

3

"Nice **skyscraper**."

Skippy Skunk has many **skills**. **Skippy Skunk** can **sketch** pictures.

2

A

SK Riddles

Listen to the riddles. Then match each riddle with the right *sk* word from the box. (Hint: Sometimes the *sk* appears at the end of the word.)

Word Box

skip	skinny	skunk	task	sky
sketch	skin	desk	skirt	skis

1 Girls might wear this instead of pants or shorts.

2 It's a job you have to do.

3 This animal can have a bad smell.

4 It's usually blue and sometimes has clouds.

5 This covers your whole body.

6 It means the same thing as *draw*.

7 It is the opposite of *fat*.

8 This is where you sit at school.

9 It rhymes with *trip*.

10 You wear these to zip down a snowy mountain.

Answers: 1. skirt 2. task 3. skunk 4. sky 5. skin 6. sketch 7. skinny 8. desk 9. skip 10. skis

15

"I hope **Skippy** doesn't **skid**."

"Brrrrr...the air is **brisk**."

Ski Lift

Skippy Skunk can **skate**. **Skippy Skunk** can **ski**.

4

B

"I have too many feet to **skip**."

"I know!" said **Skippy**. "**Skylar**, would you like to learn a new **skill**?"

"Sure," said **Skylar**.

13

Skippy wanted to thank **Skylar** for teaching him to **skip**. But how?

12

Skippy Skunk can even **skydive**! But there is one **skill Skippy** does not have.

5

Skippy sang **Skylar's skipping** song as he tried to **skip**. **Skippy** did not trip. **Skippy** did not **skin** his knee.

10

One day, a **skinny skunk** in a purple **skirt skipped** by. Her name was **Skylar**.

7

Skippy Skunk cannot **skip**! Every time **Skippy** tries to **skip**, he trips and **skins** his knee.

6

C

Skippy Skunk was **skipping**! Before long, **Skippy** was **skipping** as **skillfully** as **Skylar**!

11

"Can I **ask** you a favor?" said **Skippy**. "Will you teach me to **skip** like you?" "Sure," said **Skylar**. "That will be an easy **task**."

8

D

Then **Skylar** taught **Skippy** a special song to help him **skip**.

9

PR Cheer

Hooray for *p-r*, the best sound around!

Let's holler *p-r* words all over town!

There's **prune** and **praise** and **pride** and **propel**.

There's **pretzel** and **problem** and **price** as well.

There's **prompt** and **prize** and **proof** and **Prue**.

There's **press** and **prince** and **princess**, too.

P-r, p-r, give a great cheer,

For the **prettiest** sound you'll ever hear!

Make a list
of other *pr*
words. Then
use them in
your cheer.

16

The Princess and the Pretzel

by Violet Findley
illustrated by Richard Torrey

FAVORITE FAIRY TALES

SCHOLASTIC

After that, **Prue promised** to marry
Preston. And **Preston promised** to never,
ever put a **pretzel** in **Prue's** bed again.

Each day, **Preston** fed his pet **prairie** dog.
He **practiced** karate. He **pruned** the flowers
on his **property**.

Preston's Prize-Winning Primroses

Prince Preston

3

Phonics Fact

Pr is a blend. Blends are two consonants whose sounds are blended together when you say them. You can hear the *pr* blend at the beginning of **prince** and **Preston**. What other *pr* words can you find in this story? Look at the pictures, too!

Once upon a time, in the kingdom of **Princeton**, lived a **prince** named **Preston**.

A

PR Riddles

Listen to the riddles. Then match each riddle with the right *pr* word from the box.

Word Box

pretty	present	pry	property	prune
prince	pretzel	princess	prairie dog	prize

1. This snack is twisted and salty.
2. It means almost the same thing as *beautiful*.
3. This *pr* word rhymes with *cry*.
4. When something belongs to you, it is called this.
5. When you go to a birthday party, this is what you bring.
6. This furry wild animal lives in a hole.
7. You might get this if you win a contest.
8. The son of a king and queen is called this.
9. The daughter of a king and queen is called this.
10. This dried fruit is bigger than a raisin.

Answers: 1. pretzel 2. pretty 3. pry 4. property 5. present 6. prairie dog 7. prize 8. prince 9. princess 10. prune

---

Life was **pretty** great, except for one **problem**. **Preston** wanted to get married. But he could not find a real **princess** anywhere in **Princeton**.

B

Preston told **Prue** about his **pretzel prank** and said he was sorry. Then **Preston** **promptly proposed**.

Wow! At last, **Preston** had **proof** that **Prue** was not **pretending**. Only a real **princess** could feel a **pretzel** under 100 **pretty** quilts!

Then one stormy night, someone **pressed** **Preston's** doorbell. **Prrring, prrring!** When he opened the door, **Preston** saw a **pretty** girl!

But **Prue** did not have a good night. In fact, poor **Prue** woke up as twisted as a **pretzel**!

Elvis Presley

Preston made **Prue** some **prune** tea. Was she a real **princess** or just **pretending**? **Preston** had a **foolproof** plan to find out.

"I am **Princess Prudence**, but my friends call me **Prue**," she said. "It's **pretty** stormy. May I stay in your castle tonight?"
"Of course," said **Preston**.

6

C

The next day, **Preston** said, "I don't mean to **pry**, but how did you sleep?"
"**Pretty** badly!" proclaimed Prue. "That was **probably** the lumpiest bed in all of **Princeton**!"

11

Preston excused himself to **prepare Prue's** room. First, he put a **pretzel** on the bed. Then he covered the **pretzel** with 100 **pretty** quilts.

8

D

This bed is **pretty** high!

"Good night, **Prue**," said **Preston**.

9

CL Cheer

Hooray for *c-l*, the best sound around!

Let's holler *c-l* words all over town!

There's **cliff** and **clash** to name a few,

Clown and **clog** and **cloud** and **clue**.

There's **clock** and **club** to shout out loud,

Clean and **clang** and **clothes** and **cloud**!

C-l, *c-l*, **clap** and cheer,

For the **classiest** sound you ever will hear!

Make a list of other *cl* words. Then use them in your cheer.

Clark and Cleo's Clouds

by Elizabeth Bennett
illustrated by Kelly Kennedy

SCHOLASTIC

"Hey, Mom is pointing to a **cloud clock**. I think she wants us to **close** up our picnic basket and come home," **Cleo** told **Clark**. So they did!

CLEMENT LAKE

They **climbed** a hill and had a picnic **close** to a pretty lake.

Phonics Fact

Cl is a blend. Blends are two consonants whose sounds are blended together when you say them. You can hear the *cl* blend at the beginning of **Clark** and **Cleo**. What other *cl* words can you find in this story? Look at the pictures, too!

One day, **Clark** and his sister, **Cleo**, went to **Clovis** Park.

2

A

CL Riddles

Listen to the riddles. Then match each riddle with the right *cl* word from the box.

Word Box

clam	clown	clap	clover	close
clean	clue	climb	clock	clothes

1. You do this with your hands at the end of a play.
2. This sea creature lives in a shell.
3. It is the opposite of *dirty*.
4. It is the opposite of *open*.
5. You wear them every day.
6. You look at this to find out the time.
7. At the circus, he makes you laugh.
8. You do this to get to the top of the stairs.
9. You use this to solve a mystery.
10. If you find one with four-leaves, it will bring you luck.

15

Clark and **Cleo** thought the **clam** chowder was especially delicious!

4

B

"You see Mom!" said **Clark** with a giggle. "Very **clever**!" exclaimed Cleo.

13

Another **cluster** of **clouds** appeared.
"Guess what I see," said **Cleo**. "Here is a **clue**:
She **claps** when we **clean** our rooms."

After a while, a **cluster** of **clouds cluttered**
the **clear** sky.

I love hearing
the **clarinet**!

Another **cluster** of **clouds** appeared.
"Guess what I see," said **Clark**. "Here is
a **clue**: If you find one in a **clump** of grass,
you will have good luck."

Phonics Fact
Sometimes the *cl* can
come in the middle of a
word, as in **exclaimed**.

"You see a **clown**!" said **Cleo**.
"Very **clever**!" exclaimed Clark.

"Guess what I see," said **Clark**, staring up at the **clouds**. "Here is a **clue**: He has a round nose and **clomps** around in huge shoes."

C

"You see a four-leaf **clover**!" said **Cleo**. "Very **clever**!" exclaimed Clark.

Another **cluster** of **clouds** appeared. "Guess what I see," said **Cleo**. "Here is a **clue**: You hang them up in a **closet**."

D

"You see **clothes**!" said **Clark**. "Very **clever**!" exclaimed Cleo.

GR Cheer

Hooray for *g-r*, the best sound around!

Let's holler *g-r* words all over town!

There's **green** and **grab** and **grass** and **grandma**.

There's **grow** and **group** and **grapes** and **grandpa**.

There's **grouch** and **gray** and more words still—

Like **groan** and **greet** and **gross** and **grill**.

G-r, *g-r*, give a **great** cheer,

For the **grandest** sound you ever will hear!

> Make a list of other *gr* words. Then use them in your cheer.

A Groundhog Named Grady

by Teddy Slater
illustrated by Tammie Lyon

■SCHOLASTIC

From then on, **Grady** never **grabbed** anything again. Well, hardly ever!

Grady had a mom, a dad, a **grandma**, and a **grandpa**. He also had a big brother named **Grover** and a big sister named **Grace**.

Grady was a little **groundhog**. He lived with his family in a **great** big hole in the **ground**.

2

A

GR Riddles

Listen to the riddles. Then match each riddle with the right *gr* word from the box.

> **Word Box**
>
> grow grasshopper grapes Grace green
> gray groundhog grandma grin grass

1. There will be six more weeks of winter if this animal sees its shadow.
2. Peas are this color.
3. This fruit comes in bunches.
4. This is another word for *smile*.
5. This girl's name rhymes with *place*.
6. This grows all over the ground.
7. Little Red Riding Hood went to visit her.
8. When you water a plant, it does this.
9. You get this color when you mix black and white paint.
10. This green insect likes to jump.

They all thought **Grady** was the **greatest** little **groundhog** in the world. Except for one thing. . . .

4

B

"Poor **Grady**!" cried **Grace**, **Grover**, Mom, Dad, **Grandma**, and **Grandpa** all together. No one said, "That's what you get for **grabbing**." They didn't have to.

13

Grady was a **grabber**! **Grady grabbed** all the **grapes** out of **Grandma's** fruit bowl.

And **Grady** was always **grabbing Grover's** toy **grizzly** bear.

But it was too late. **Grady grabbed** the thorny stem.
"OUCH!" **Grady groaned**.

One day, **Grady's** whole family went for a **group** walk in **Greenwood Grove**.

Grady grabbed Grace's green balloon.

C

A **great** big rosebush was **growing** by a **gravel** path. **Grady** reached out to **grab** a flower. "Be careful!" **Grandma** warned.

Once **Grady** even **grabbed Grandpa's** whiskers. "Ouch!" **Grandpa groaned**.

D

"**Grady**," **Grandpa grumbled**, "would you please stop **grabbing** everything!" But **Grady** just **grinned**. Then he **grabbed Grandma's** glasses.

FL Cheer

Hooray for *f-l*, the best sound around!

Let's holler *f-l* words all over town!

There's **flap** and **flop** and **flower** and **flu.**

There's **fluff** and **flamingo** and **flutter**, too!

There's **fly** and **flock** and **float** and **floor.**

There's **flute** and **flag** and many more!

F-l, *f-l*, give a great cheer,

For the most **flawless** sound you ever will hear!

> Make a list of other *fl* words. Then use them in your cheer.

Flora Flamingo Learns to Fly

by Maria Fleming
illustrated by Kellie Lewis

SCHOLASTIC

'Bye, **Floyd** and my bug friends! I'm **flying** to **Florida.**

Have fun in **Florida, Flora!**

Soon it is time for all the **flamingos** to **fly** to **Florida.** Who will lead the **flock**? **Flora**, of course! And her **flying** is **FLAWLESS**!

Flap! Flap! Flap!

Flop!

Every day, **Flora** tries to **fly** but fails.
Flap, flap, flap…**flop. Flap, flap, flap**…**flop.**

I wish I could **fly** like the other **flamingos**.

Phonics Fact

Fl is a blend. Blends are two consonants whose sounds are blended together when you say them. You can hear the *fl* blend at the beginning of **fluffy**, **Flora**, **flamingo**, and **fly**. What other *fl* words can you find in this story? Look at the pictures, too!

Fluffy little **Flora Flamingo** cannot **fly**.

2   A

Listen to the riddles. Then match each riddle with the right *fl* word from the box.

Word Box

float	flamingo	flop	flapjack	flounder
flowers	Florida	flash	flap	flock

1 You put these in a vase.

2 This kind of bird is big and pink.

3 A firefly's light does this at night.

4 This is a state in our country.

5 Boats do this on water.

6 It rhymes with *stop*.

7 This is what a group of birds is called.

8 It is another word for *pancake*.

9 This is a kind of fish.

10 Birds do this with their wings to fly.

Answers: 1. flowers 2. flamingo 3. flash 4. Florida 5. float 6. flop 7. flock 8. flapjack 9. flounder 10. flap

15

Florida, here we come!

Flora is upset. She wants to **fly** to the **flamingo** festival in **Florida** with the rest of the **flamingo flock**.

4   B

Look, **Floyd**! I'm **flying**! I'M **FLYING**!!!

Yay, **Flora**!

Flap, flap, flap, flap, flap, flap!
They do! **Flora** is not a **flop** at **flying** after all!

13

Flap! Flap! Flap!

Keep **flapping**, **Flora**!

Will the feathers help **Flora fly**?
Flap, flap, flap…

I wish I could **fly** like the **butterflies** can **fly**.

Phonics Fact
Sometimes the *fl* blend comes in the middle of a word, as in **butterflies**. Can you spot another word in this story that has the *fl* blend in the middle? (Answer: **fireflies**)

Flora watches the **butterflies**.
They **flutter** from **flower** to **flower**.

Your wings are not **flimsy**, **Flora**.

"Just be patient," says **Floyd**. "Soon you will **fly** like the rest of the **flamingo flock**." **Flora** hopes **Floyd** is right.

I wish I could **fly** like the **fireflies** can **fly**.

At night, **Flora** watches the **fireflies**. They **flicker** and **flash** as they **flit** through the air.

Flora tries to **fly** like the **butterflies**.
But it's no use.
Flap, flap, flap…**flop. Flap, flap, flap**…**flop.**

6

C

Flora tries to **fly** like the **fireflies**.
But it's no use.
Flap, flap, flap…**flop. Flap, flap, flap**…**flop.**

8

D

One morning, **Flora** wakes up. Her **fluff** is gone!
Now she has **flashy** pink feathers!

11

Flora's friend **Floyd Flounder floats** by.
"I'm a **flop** at **flying**," **Flora** tells **Floyd**.

9

TR Cheer

Hooray for *t-r*, the best sound around!

Let's holler *t-r* words all over town!

There's **troll** and **trip** and **tree** and **true**.

There's **truck** and **train** and **treasure**, too!

There's **track** and **treat** and **trash** and **tray**.

There's **trot** and **trick** and **trap**—hooray!

T-r, *t-r*, give a great cheer,

For the most **tremendous** sound you ever will hear!

> Make a list of other *tr* words. Then use them in your cheer.

16

The Trolls Take a Trip

by Maria Fleming
illustrated by Doug Jones

SCHOLASTIC

Then the **trolls travel** home with memories to **treasure**. They would not **trade** their **tradition** for anything—not even a **trillion** dollars!

14

The **trolls travel** to Lake **Trout** from near and far.

3

The **trolls** have a **tradition**. Every summer, they make a **trip** to Lake **Trout**.

A

TR Riddles

Listen to the riddles. Then match each riddle with the right *tr* word from the box.

Word Box

trip	treat	train	tree	trumpet
tractor	trout	trolley	trophy	tray

1. This is something tall that grows.
2. You find this vehicle on a farm.
3. It rhymes with *jolly*.
4. This is a kind of fish.
5. You play music on this.
6. It is something tasty to eat.
7. This moves along tracks.
8. This is flat and you carry things on it.
9. It rhymes with *rip*.
10. This is a kind of prize.

Answers: 1. tree 2. tractor 3. trolley 4. trout 5. trumpet 6. treat 7. train 8. tray 9. trip 10. trophy

They **travel** by **truck** and **trailer**.

B

They get back onto the **trains**, **trolleys**, and **tractors**.

At the end of the **trip**, the **trolls** get back into their **trucks** and **trailers**.

They **travel** by **train** and by **trolley**. Some **trolls** even **travel** by **tractor**!

At night, the **trolls** play **trumpets** and **trombones**.

The **trolls** fish in Lake **Trout**.

The **trolls** bring **trays** of **treats**. They have a picnic under the **trees**.

6

C

The **trolls** sing and dance. They have **tremendous** fun.

11

The **trolls** play games and **try** to win **trophies**.

8

D

Their favorite game is racing **tricycles** around a **track**.

9

SL Cheer

Hooray for *s-l*, the best sound around!

Let's holler *s-l* words all over town!

There's **sloth** and **sled** and **slush** and **sleek**.

There's **slug** and **slide** and **slap** and **sleep**.

There's **slip** and **slope** and **slug** and **sly**.

There's **slice** and **slow** and **slink**, oh my!

S-l, *s-l*, give a great cheer,

For the **slickest** sound you ever will hear!

Make a list of other *sl* words. Then use them in your cheer.

---

sl

Sleepyhead Sloth

by Violet Findley
illustrated by Doug Jones

■ SCHOLASTIC

I do so love **sleepovers**!

Then **Sloth** says, "Let me get my **slippers**. I do so love **sleepovers**!"

Sloth
1 Slick Road
Sleepytown
the Rain Forest

Rise and shine, **Sleepyhead**!

Slinky tries everything to wake **Sloth** from his **slumber**.

Meet **Sloth**. Meet his pal, **Slinky**.

A

SL Riddles

Listen to the riddles. Then match each riddle with the right *sl* word from the box.

Word Box				
sloth	sleep	slick	sled	slippers
slurp	sloppy	slice	slow	slide

1. You use this to slide down snowy hills.
2. It is the opposite of *fast*.
3. You slip down this at the playground.
4. You put these on your feet at night.
5. A piece of pizza is sometimes called this.
6. Babies do this in their cribs.
7. It is the opposite of *neat*.
8. This word rhymes with *click*.
9. This slow-moving animal lives in the rainforest.
10. It is not polite to drink this way.

Answers: 1. sled 2. slow 3. slide 4. slippers 5. slice 6. sleep 7. sloppy 8. slick 9. sloth 10. slurp

Slinky slithers over in **slick** sunglasses and starts playing the bongo drums. **Slap! Slap! Slap!**

B

Sloth opens his eyes a **sliver** and **slowly** smiles.

Then **Slinky** adds **slyly**, "Did I mention that it's a **SLEEPOVER** party?"

But **sleepyhead Sloth** keeps snoozing!

Slinky slithers over and shouts, "Wake up, **Sloth**! I'm having a party in my tree!"

But **sleepyhead Sloth** keeps snoozing!

Slinky slithers over and offers Sloth a slurp of his milkshake and a big sloppy slice of pizza.

6

C

But sleepyhead Sloth keeps snoozing!

11

Slinky slides over and invites Sloth to go sledding on Slippery Slope with their slug friend named Slimy.

8

D

But sleepyhead Sloth keeps snoozing!

9

CH Cheer

Hooray for *c-h*, the best sound around!

Let's holler *c-h* words all over town!

There's **chimp** and **chick** and **chair** and **chore**.

There's **charm** and **child** and so many more—

Like **chip** and **cheese** and **brunch** and **lunch**

And **rich** and **peach** and **munch** and **crunch**!

C-h, *c-h*, give a great **cheer**,

For the most **charming** sound you ever will hear!

Make a list of other words that have *ch* at the beginning or the end. Then use them in your cheer.

Chimp and Chick's Lunch

by Liza Charlesworth
illustrated by Jannie Ho

SCHOLASTIC

"Mmmm! What a **charming** meal!" **cheeped** Chick.
"Yes," **chuckled** Chimp. "It's the best **lunch** I have ever **munched**!"

Chipmunk came by yesterday!

I'm a **checkers** champ!

CHESS
CHECKERS

Chuck's MAGIC Cheeseburger

Chimp and **Chick chatted**. They played **chess** and **checkers**. They read a **chapter** book. All of this made the two **chums** very hungry!

> Hi, **Chick**!

Phonics Fact

Ch is a digraph. Digraphs are two letters put together to make a single sound, such as the *ch* sound in **chilly**, **chick**, and **chimp**. What other *ch* words can you find in this story? Look at the pictures, too!

One **chilly** day, **Chick** went to visit his **chum**, **Chimp**.

A

CH Riddles

Listen to the riddles. Then match each with the right *ch* word from the box. (Hint: Sometimes the *ch* appears at the end of the word.)

Word Box

chick	cheese	cherry	checkers	chair
chuckle	chimp	chilly	lunch	crunch

1. This is another name for *monkey*.
2. It means almost the same thing as *laugh*.
3. This sweet, red fruit is small with a long stem.
4. One person can sit on it.
5. You eat this meal in the middle of the day.
6. People put this on top of pizza and burgers.
7. This sound is made when you bite into an apple.
8. This board game has red and black playing pieces.
9. It means almost the same thing as *cold*.
10. This is the name for a baby chicken.

Answers: 1. chimp 2. chuckle 3. cherry 4. chair 5. lunch 6. cheese 7. crunch 8. checkers 9. chilly 10. chick

---

Phonics Fact

The digraph *ch* can also appear at the end of a word such as **lunch**. Can you find another word on this page that ends in *ch*? Check the rest of the book, too! (Answer: **munch**)

So **Chimp** and **Chick** decided to make some **lunch**.
"What should we **munch**?" cheeped Chick.
"You **choose**," answered **Chimp**.

B

> **Crunch!**

Chimp poured some **punch**. Then the two **chums** plopped down in **chairs** and shared the **sandwich**. Crunch, crunch, crunch, crunch!

Chick took the **cheddar cheese** and **cherries** and **chili** and **chips** and **chestnuts** and **chocolate** and made a huge **sandwich**!

"OK," cheeped Chick. "I **choose** **cheddar cheese**!"
So **Chimp** got **cheddar cheese**.

"I **choose** **chocolate**!" cheeped Chick.
So **Chimp** got **chocolate**.

"I **choose** **chili**!" cheeped Chick.
So **Chimp** got **chili**.

"I **choose cherries**!" **cheeped Chick**.
So **Chimp** got **cherries**.

C

"This food looks delicious," said **Chimp cheerfully**.
"But how do we turn it into our **lunch**?"
"I have an idea!" **cheeped Chick**.

"I **choose chips**!" **cheeped Chick**.
So **Chimp** got **chips**.

D

"I **choose chestnuts**!" **cheeped Chick**.
So **Chimp** got **chestnuts**.

SH Cheer

Hooray for *s-h*, the best sound around!

Let's holler *s-h* words all over town!

There's **shoe** and **shelf** and **splash** and **wish**.

There's **shop** and **shirt** and **push** and **fish**.

There's **shell** and **shorts** and **crush** and **dash**.

There's **shape** and **ship** and **shout** and **smash**.

S-h, *s-h*, give a great cheer,

For the **shiniest** sound you ever will hear!

Make a list of other words that have *sh* at the beginning or the end. Then use them in your cheer.

Phonics Tales!

sh

Shelly's New Shoes

by Pamela Chanko
illustrated by Doug Jones

■ SCHOLASTIC

Cash or charge?

SHOELACES

SHULTZ'S SNEAKERS THEY'RE SHARP

"I know. They are really **sharp**!" **gushed Shelly**. "We'll take the red **shoes**," said Mom to the **shopkeeper**. "Isn't that a **shock**?"

Sheep
by Shelly

Shark!
by Shelly

Shelly also has some favorite **shoes**. **She** thinks they are really **sharp**!

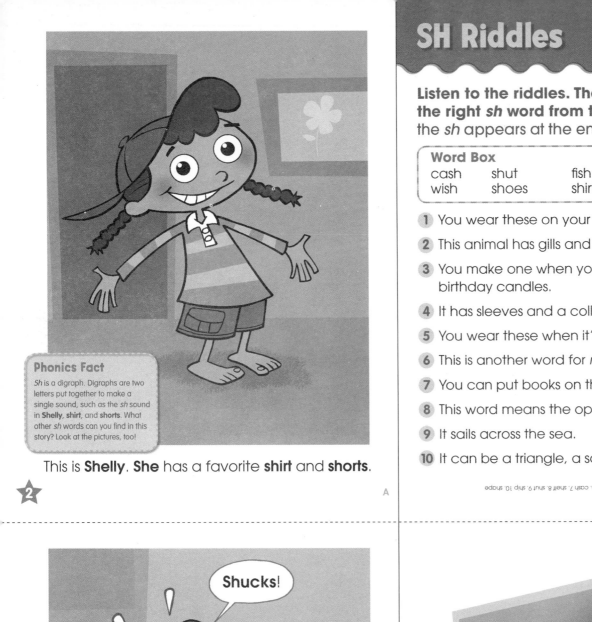

This is **Shelly**. **She** has a favorite **shirt** and **shorts**.

2

A

SH Riddles

Listen to the riddles. Then match each with the right *sh* word from the box. (Hint: Sometimes the *sh* appears at the end of the word.)

Word Box				
cash	shut	fish	shelf	shorts
wish	shoes	shirt	ship	shape

1 You wear these on your feet.

2 This animal has gills and swims.

3 You make one when you blow out your birthday candles.

4 It has sleeves and a collar.

5 You wear these when it's too hot for long pants.

6 This is another word for *money*.

7 You can put books on this.

8 This word means the opposite of *open*.

9 It sails across the sea.

10 It can be a triangle, a square, or a circle.

Answers: 1. shoes 2. fish 3. wish 4. shirt 5. shorts 6. cash 7. shelf 8. shut 9. ship 10. shape

15

> **Shucks!**

One day, **Shelly** got a **shock**. She **pushed** and **shoved** her feet into her **shoes**. But her **shoes** did not fit!

4

B

But then **Shelly** spotted one last pair on the top **shelf** in the **shadows**.
"**Gosh**," said Mom, "those look just like your old **shoes**!"

13

Shelly shut her eyes and **shed** a tear.
"I **wish** I didn't need new **shoes**!" **she** cried.

⭐ 12

Phonics Fact
Sometimes the *sh* sound comes at the end of a word, as in **trash**.

"These **shoes** are going in the **trash**!" Mom said.
"No!" **shouted Shelly**.

⭐ 5

SHOES THAT MAKE A SPLASH!

Next, he **showed Shelly** some sandals covered in **seashells**.
"These **crush** my toes!" **she** said.

⭐ 10

FRESH NEW FASHIONS!

"I have many **shoes** to **show** you," said the **shopkeeper**. "We have **shelves** and **shelves** of **shoes**!"

⭐ 7

"We **should** go **shopping**," Mom said. So **she** grabbed **Shelly** and **dashed** to **Sherman's** **shoe shop**.

6

C

Shelly tried on every **shoe** in the **shop**. But the **shoes** were either too **showy**, or too **shaky**, or they gave her a **rash**.

11

First, he **showed Shelly** some fancy **shoes**. "Too **shiny**!" **she** said.

8

D

Then, he **showed Shelly** some pointy **shoes**. "I don't like the **shape**!" **she** said.

9

TH Cheer

Hooray for *t-h*, the best sound around!

Let's holler *t-h* words all over town!

There's **thump** and **thing** and **teeth** and **mouth**.

There's **thumb** and **thorn** and **north** and **south**.

There's **thread** and **throat** and **bath** and **moth**.

There's **think** and **thank** and **math** and **cloth**.

T-h, *t-h*, give a great cheer,

For the most **thrilling** sound you ever will hear!

> Make a list of other words that have *th* at the beginning or the end. Then use them in your cheer.

16

Phonics Tales!

th

The Thing That Went Thump

by Maria Fleming
illustrated by Stephen Lewis

Thump! Thump! Thud!

■ SCHOLASTIC

Youth Soccer League

I promise, **Theo**.

Thanks, **Ruth**.

But he made **Ruth** take an **oath** that she would never scare him like that again.

14

Seth's Toothpaste

Minty Breath Mouthwash

Bertha's Bubble Bath

> **Phonics Fact**
> The digraph *th* can also appear at the end of a word, as in **bath** and **teeth**.

So **Theo** took a **bath**, brushed his **teeth**, and went to bed early.

3

One **Thursday** night, **Theo Thorn** was very sleepy.

A

TH Riddles

Listen to the riddles. Then match each with the right *th* word from the box. (Hint: Sometimes the *th* appears at the end of the word.)

Word Box

Earth	thump	sloth	thorn	bath
Thursday	three	teeth	math	thick

1. This day comes after Wednesday.
2. This is something very pointy.
3. You need these to chew food.
4. This is the opposite of *thin*.
5. This is the planet we live on.
6. This animal moves very slowly.
7. You take this to get clean.
8. You use numbers to do this subject.
9. This loud sound rhymes with *bump*.
10. This number comes after *two*.

Answers: 1. Thursday 2. thorn 3. teeth 4. thick 5. Earth 6. sloth 7. bath 8. math 9. thump 10. three

Suddenly, **Theo** heard a strange sound.
Thump! Thump! Thud! Thump! Thump! Thud!

B

"Okay," said **Theo**.
Theo was **thankful** the **thumping thing** was only his sister.

"Sorry, **Theo**," said **Ruth**. "Will you help me **with** my **math** homework?"

What could it be? **Theo thought** of a **thousand** scary **things**.

I'll **throw** this shoe if it comes **through** the door.

Theo hid **beneath** the covers. He held his **breath**. Suddenly, the door burst open. In **thumped** . . .

I could squeeze **through** if I were **thinner**.

Maybe it was a wooly **mammoth** with big **teeth**. **Thump! Thump! Thud!**

Maybe it was a giant **sloth with thick** fur.
Thump! **Thump**! **Thud**!

6   C

...**Theo's** sister!
"**Ruth**, you scared me to **death**!" said **Theo**.

11

Maybe it was a monster **with three** heads and
thirty eyes. **Thump**! **Thump**! **Thud**!

8   D

Phonics Fact

Sometimes the letters *th* make
a sound that is a little different
from the sound in **thump**. Say the
words *the, that,* and *this.* Can you
hear how the *th* sounds different?
Be on the lookout for both kinds of
th words in the rest of this story.

THUMP! **THUMP**! **THUD**! **THUMP**! **THUMP**! **THUD**!
The **thumping thing** was getting closer!

9